How to Draw the Life and Times of
George H. W. Bush

Lewis K. Parker

The Rosen Publishing Group's
PowerKids Press™
New York

This book is dedicated to my family, especially to Dakota, Tyrus, and Nicholas.

Published in 2006 by The Rosen Publishing Group, Inc.
29 East 21st Street, New York, NY 10010

First Edition

Editor: Melissa Acevedo and Amelie von Zumbusch
Layout Design: Julio A. Gil
Photo Researcher: Nicole DiMella

Illustrations: All illustrations by Albert B. Hanner.
Photo Credits: pp. 4, 9, 10 George Bush Presidential Library; p. 7 © Wally McNamee/Corbis; p. 8 Courtesy
John Vaughn and Catherine Athearn; p. 12 © AP Photo; p. 14 (both) Manuscripts and Archives, Yale University
Library; pp. 18, 26 © Bettmann/Corbis; p. 20 Courtesy of the Ronald Reagan Library; p. 22 Courtesy Map
Resources; p. 24 © AP Photo/DOD; p. 28 National Portrait Gallery, Smithsonian Institution/Art Resource, NY.

Library of Congress Cataloging-in-Publication Data

Parker, Lewis K.
  How to draw the life and times of George H.W. Bush / Lewis K. Parker.— 1st ed.
    p. cm. — (A kid's guide to drawing the presidents of the United States of America)
  Includes bibliographical references and index.
  ISBN 1-4042-3017-3 (library binding : alk. paper)
  1. Bush, George, 1924– —Juvenile literature. 2. Presidents—United States—Biography—Juvenile literature. 3.
Drawing—Technique—Juvenile literature. I. Title. II. Series.
  E882.P37 2007
  973.931092—dc22

                              2005026680

Printed in China

Contents

Preparing for the Presidency

George Herbert Walker Bush, the forty-first president of the United States, was born in Milton, Massachusetts, on June 12, 1924. When he was about one year old, his family moved to Greenwich, Connecticut. When he was 13, Bush went to Phillips

Academy in Andover, Massachusetts. During Bush's last year there, America entered World War II. World War II had started in 1939 when Germany attacked Poland, another European country. America stayed out of the war until Japan, Germany's ally, attacked a U.S. naval base in Pearl Harbor, Hawaii, on December 7, 1941. In June 1942, Bush graduated from Phillips Academy and joined the U.S. Navy. By June 9, 1943, he had completed his training and had become a pilot in the navy.

The war ended in August 1945. In September 1945, Bush entered Yale University in New Haven, Connecticut. He graduated in 1948, and moved to

Texas. In 1964, Bush ran for the U.S. Senate but lost. He was a member of the Republican Party, which supported lower taxes. He was elected to the U.S. House of Representatives in 1966 and in 1968. In 1971, he became the U.S. ambassador to the United Nations. From 1974 to 1976, he represented America in China. From 1976 to 1977, he was the head of the Central Intelligence Agency (CIA). In 1980, Bush became Ronald Reagan's running mate in the presidential election. They were elected and Bush served as vice president for eight years. In 1988, Bush ran for president and won.

You will need the following supplies to draw the life and times of George H. W. Bush:

✓ A sketch pad   ✓ An eraser   ✓ A pencil   ✓ A ruler

These are some of the shapes and drawing terms you need to know:

Horizontal Line	——	Squiggly Line	∿
Oval	⬭	Trapezoid	▱
Rectangle	▭	Triangle	△
Shading	▬	Vertical Line		
Slanted Line	/	Wavy Line	∿

President George H. W. Bush

George H. W. Bush was sworn in on January 20, 1989. One of Bush's early challenges was deciding what to do about Manuel Noriega, the dictator of Panama, a Central American country. The U.S. government had proof that Noriega was shipping illegal drugs into America. Bush quickly sent soldiers to capture Noriega. He surrendered, or gave up, and was taken to the United States. There he was found guilty of drug smuggling and sentenced to 40 years in prison.

In 1990, Saddam Hussein, the dictator of Iraq, a country in the Middle East, attacked Kuwait, a small country near Iraq. In 1991, Bush sent U.S. forces to Kuwait, and the Persian Gulf War began. The war lasted fewer than two months, and Hussein pulled his troops out of Kuwait.

Bush ran for reelection in 1992. Because of the failing economy, his popularity had decreased and he was not reelected. Bush retired to Houston, Texas.

A few weeks after the beginning of the Persian Gulf War, President George H. W. Bush visited American troops in Barstow, California. Bush praised the soldiers' hard work and told them, "America must always be prepared to fight for freedom and security."

George H. W. Bush's Texas

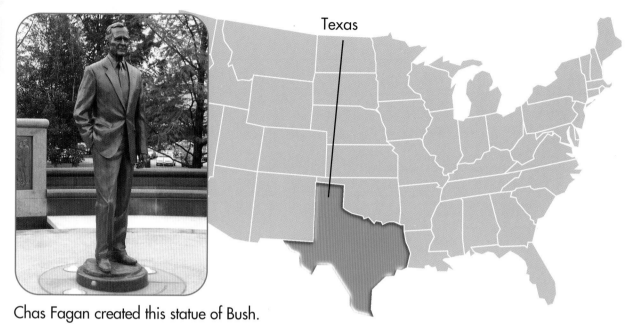

Chas Fagan created this statue of Bush.

Texas

Map of the United States of America

Although George H. W. Bush was born in Massachusetts and grew up in Connecticut, he called Texas home for most of his adult life. He also retired to Houston, Texas, after leaving politics. The state of Texas has honored Bush in several ways. People going to Texas may fly into the George Bush Intercontinental Airport, about 23 miles (37 km) from downtown Houston, Texas. Upon entering the airport, people are greeted by a 7-foot (2 m) bronze statue of Bush.

A monument honoring Bush, shown here, was built in downtown Houston in 2004. The monument cost $1.7 million to build. It includes a semicircular wall that has engravings, or carvings. They honor Bush's service in the navy, his presidency, and his family. In the middle of the monument is an 8-foot (2.4 m), 650-pound (295 kg) bronze statue of Bush.

The George Bush Presidential Library and Museum is located on the grounds of Texas A&M University in College Station, Texas. The library and museum, which opened in 1997, covers 90 acres (36 h). The library houses Bush's speeches, letters, and other writings, as well as more than two million photographs and 5,000 videotapes. The museum's exhibits highlight the forces and challenges that shaped Bush's life from his childhood to his presidency.

The George Bush Presidential Library and Museum, seen above, opened in November 1997.

Growing Up and Going to War

On June 12, 1924, George H. W. Bush was born in the house shown at right, in Milton, Massachusetts. He was the second of five children. In  1925, the Bush family moved to Greenwich, Connecticut, about 25 miles (40 km) from New York City, where Bush's father worked as a banker. Bush attended Greenwich Country Day School. In 1937, he went to Phillips Academy in Andover, Massachusetts. He became captain of the school's baseball team and president of the senior class.

Bush was a senior at Phillips Academy when America entered World War II, in 1941. When Bush graduated in 1942, he joined the U.S. Navy and became a fighter pilot. He served on the aircraft carrier USS *San Jacinto*, in the Pacific Ocean. An aircraft carrier is a ship that allows aircraft to take off from its deck. During the war Bush flew in more than 50 battles. For bravery in action, he was given the Distinguished Flying Cross prize.

1

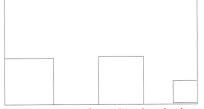

Begin your picture of Bush's birthplace by drawing a large rectangle. Add four vertical lines and four horizontal lines to make two squares and a rectangle inside the large rectangle as shown.

2

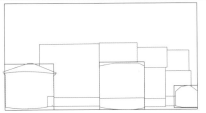

Look carefully at the drawing and draw the shapes inside of the small rectangle and the squares you made in step 1. Then use horizontal and vertical lines to draw nine shapes as shown.

3

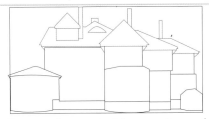

Erase all extra lines. Add two triangular shapes as shown. Add lines to make a rectangle below the left shape. Draw the roof, paying close attention to the corners. Add four chimneys and a curved shape.

4

Erase all extra lines. Add shapes to the middle of the house as shown. Add horizontal and slanted lines to the house's roof and side. Add details to the porch on the left and the shed on the right.

5

Add three vertical lines and two curved lines to the big window in the middle of the house. Add a curved line to the roof as shown. Then add 19 windows to the house as shown.

6

Add a horizontal line and a vertical line to the big window. Add a rectangle with a line through the middle of it to 14 of the other windows. Add details to two of the chimneys.

7

Draw five drainpipes as shown. The drainpipe on the left branches into two parts. Add 10 squares and two rectangles under the big window as shown.

8

Erase any extra lines. Now shade your drawing of George H. W. Bush's birthplace.

Barbara Pierce Bush

Barbara Pierce was born in Rye, New York, on June 8, 1925. Bush met Barbara in December 1941, at a Christmas dance in Greenwich, Connecticut. She was 16 years old. The two liked each other immediately. During his time in the U.S. Navy, Bush and Barbara stayed in touch by writing letters.

On January 6, 1945, Bush and Barbara married. Soon after the wedding, they moved to Virginia Beach, Virginia, where Bush trained new pilots. When the war ended in 1945, the couple moved to New Haven, Connecticut, where Bush attended Yale University. They later moved to Texas in 1948. The Bushes had six children. One of their children died from an illness while still very young.

While her husband was president, Barbara supported many important causes, including the encouragement of literacy. She helped found the Barbara Bush Foundation for Family Literacy in 1989.

1 The picture of Barbara Pierce Bush on page 12 was taken in 1943, when she was a student at Ashley Hall in Charleston, South Carolina. Begin your drawing of her with a large rectangle.

2 Draw a slanted oval as the guide for her head. Use slanted lines to draw the guide for her neck and body. Add more slanted lines to draw the guides for her arms as shown.

3 Draw the outlines of her hair, her face, her neck, her necklace, and her body with wavy lines. Add three circles and a line as guides for her nose, her eyes, and her mouth.

4 Use the guides to draw her lips, her nose, her eyes, and her eyebrows. Add squiggly lines to show her body and upper arms. Use the guides to draw her folded arms and her hand.

5 Erase all the guides, except for the large rectangular guide from step 1.

6 Draw wavy lines for the waves in her hair. Add more wavy lines for the folds in her clothing. Draw a small circle in each of her eyes.

7 Finish drawing Barbara Bush's necklace with a lot of tiny circles. As you get closer to her shoulders, you can use squiggly lines instead.

8 Erase all extra lines. You are now ready to shade the drawing of Mrs. Bush. Her mouth, her dress, and her hair are the darkest parts.

From College to the Oil Business

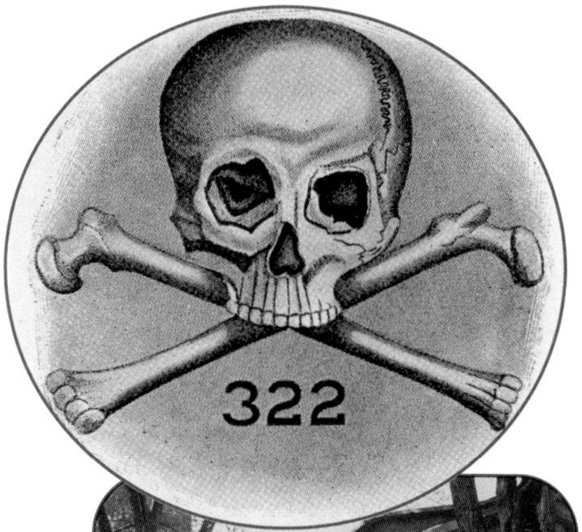

At Yale University George H. W. Bush majored in economics. He was an excellent student. He also joined Skull and Bones, a secret club, which met in the building shown at right. The club's symbol is shown above. Bush graduated from Yale in 1948.

In 1948, Bush took a job with an oil company and moved his family to Odessa, Texas. At first he worked sweeping floors and painting machinery. In 1950, Bush and his friend John Overbey started a company to buy and sell land that had oil. That same year the Bushes moved to Midland, Texas. In 1953, Bush and Overbey combined their company with another company to form the Zapata Petroleum Corporation. In 1954, a new branch of the company called Zapata Off-Shore started drilling for oil in the Gulf of Mexico. In 1959, Bush bought Zapata Off-Shore and moved it and his family to Houston, Texas.

322

1

Begin your drawing of the Skull and Bones symbol by making a large rectangular guide. A skull is the group of bones in an animal's head that protects its brain.

2

Draw a circle near the top of the rectangular guide. Draw two smaller circles and an oval as guides for the eye and nose holes. Draw two long, slanted rectangles with curved ends as shown.

3

Look carefully at the drawing and draw the shape of the skull. Then use the slanted rectangular guides from step 2 to draw the crossed bones.

4

Erase all extra lines, including the rectangular guide from step 1.

5

Draw the holes for the eyes and nose with squiggly lines. Draw nine slanted lines below the nose and nine teeth. Use squiggly lines to add details to both sides of the skull.

6

Erase all extra lines. Look carefully at the drawing and add details to the ends of the bones.

7

Below the skull and the bones, write the number 322.

8

Use shading to finish your drawing of the Skull and Bones symbol. The holes for the eyes and the nose are the darkest parts.

Getting Involved in Politics

Three years after moving to Houston, Texas, George H. W. Bush became chairman of the Harris County Republican Party. In 1964, he ran for U.S. senator but lost. In 1966

and 1968, he was elected to the U.S. House of Representatives by the people of Houston. Houston's flag is shown above. In 1970, he ran for senator again but lost.

From 1971 to 1973, Bush served as the U.S. ambassador to the United Nations. In 1973, President Richard Nixon named Bush chair of the Republican National Committee. During this time Nixon was involved in the Watergate scandal. A group of men had broken into the Democratic Party headquarters in the Watergate Hotel in Washington, D.C. Nixon said he didn't know about the break-in, but there was proof that he had lied. Bush had supported Nixon, but when he learned Nixon had lied, he signed a letter asking Nixon to resign. Two days later Nixon resigned.

1

The flag of Houston, Texas, has a train engine on it because Houston was once a major railroad center. Begin the drawing of the Houston train engine with a rectangular guide.

2

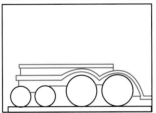

Draw a long rectangle along the bottom of the rectangular guide. Draw two circles on top of the left side of the rectangle. Draw two slightly larger rectangles on top of the right side of the rectangle.

3

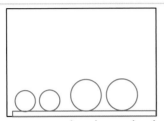

Draw a long rectangle. Draw two lines that go straight over the small circles, curve around the bigger circles, and touch the rectangular guide. Add four vertical lines and four horizontal lines as shown.

4

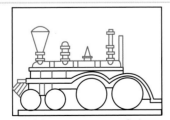

Draw a curved line on top of the rectangle from step 3. Draw five shapes crossing the line as shown. Four of them are made up of many different shapes. Add 12 vertical lines. Draw the shapes on the far left.

5

Draw two horizontal lines and a curved line from the tall shape on the right to the edge of the rectangular guide. Add four rectangles. Use curved lines to fill in the space below these rectangles.

6

Draw two circles and 16 straight lines inside both small circles. Draw a long rectangle with curved ends between the big circles. Add 14 short straight lines and two curved lines inside each big circle.

7

Erase all extra lines. Use wavy lines to draw two puffs of smoke as shown. Use more wavy lines to add details to the puff of smoke on the left.

8

Finish your drawing with shading. You can leave the stripes on the side and parts of the wheels blank.

From the CIA and China to Vice President

Gerald Ford, President Nixon's vice president, became president when Nixon resigned. In 1974, President Ford let Bush choose among several appointments. Bush asked to be sent to China, a  Communist country, as the U.S. representative. He served there from October 1974 to January 1976. In 1976, President Ford appointed Bush head of the CIA. In 1977, when President Jimmy Carter, a Democrat, took office, Bush resigned from the CIA. He and his family moved from Washington, D.C., back to Houston, Texas. For two years Bush held a number of different jobs outside of politics.

On May 1, 1979, Bush announced that he was a candidate for the 1980 presidential election. Unfortunately for Bush Ronald Reagan was the Republicans' more popular candidate. In late May, Bush withdrew from the race. However, Reagan chose him as his vice-presidential running mate.

1

You can see a picture of the CIA seal on page 18. Start drawing your own picture of the seal by making a large circle.

2

Inside the circle draw two slightly smaller circles. In the middle of the circles use a horizontal line and two wavy lines to draw the shape of a shield.

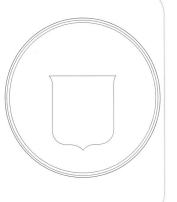

3

Look carefully at the drawing and draw an eagle's head. Inside the shield draw a vertical line, a horizontal line, and two slanted lines that all cross at the same point.

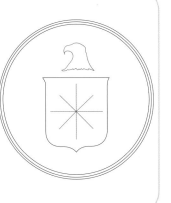

4

Add wide *V*'s between the horizontal and vertical lines. Draw narrow *V*'s around the slanted lines. Add eight small *V*'s. Add the eagle's eye and beak. Draw feathers.

5

Draw six squiggly shapes below the eagle. Draw two curved lines below the shield. Look at the drawing and add the squiggly shapes connecting the ends of the two curved lines.

6

Write the words "UNITED STATES OF AMERICA" in between the two curved lines you drew in step 5. Remember to use all capital letters.

7

At the top of the circle, write the words "CENTRAL INTELLIGENCE AGENCY" in capital letters.

8

You can now shade in your drawing of the CIA seal. Look at the drawing shown here and the picture on page 18 for help.

Serving as Vice President

On January 20, 1981, George H. W. Bush became the vice president under President Ronald Reagan. Reagan and Bush are shown here. On March 30, 1981, a man named John W. Hinckley Jr. shot President Reagan. While Reagan healed from the wound,  Bush carried out the duties of the president. When Reagan recovered, he gave Bush more responsibility. One of Bush's new jobs was to supervise, or oversee, a group that included navy and air force members. The group was trying to stop illegal drugs from coming into the United States.

Bush was Reagan's running mate again in 1984. They won the election. On July 13, 1985, Reagan had to have an operation. While Reagan was recovering, Bush took over the presidency as required by the U.S. Constitution. This was the first time that a vice president had taken over for a president in this kind of situation.

1 The picture on page 20 shows President Ronald Reagan standing next to Vice President George H. W. Bush. Begin your drawing of Reagan with a large rectangular guide.

2 Draw an oval at the top of the rectangular guide. Use seven slanted lines to draw the guide for his body. Add four ovals and two circles as guides for his arms and his hands.

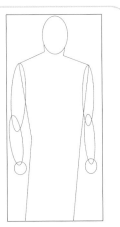

3 Draw the shapes of his hair, his ears, and his chin. Add three circles and a curved shape as guides for his eyes, his nose, and his mouth. Draw his collar and his open jacket with curved lines.

4 Use the guides to draw his eyes, his eyebrows, his nose, and his mouth. Draw his tie and his jacket's collar. Add wavy lines for waves in his hair, a fold in his tie, and wrinkles in his skin.

5 Draw his arms and hands as shown. Use the guides to draw the outline of his body and his legs. Add curving lines to separate his legs and the two sides of his jacket.

6 Erase all extra lines, including the rectangular guide from step 1.

7 Use wavy and slanted lines to add details to his jacket. Draw three small circles for buttons. Add a small shape for the handkerchief in his pocket.

8 You can now shade in your drawing of Ronald Reagan. His hair should be the darkest part of the picture.

President Bush and the "War on Drugs"

On October 12, 1987, George H. W. Bush announced that he would run in the 1988

presidential election. Some people thought he had been involved in the Iran-Contra scandal. The U.S. government had been secretly selling weapons to Iran to help that country in its war against Iraq. Money from these sales was then used illegally. It went to help a group called the Contras overthrow the government of Nicaragua, a Central American country. Bush said that he had not been involved, and the Republicans chose him as their presidential candidate. He won the election and was sworn in on January 20, 1989.

One of President Bush's first challenges was dealing with the illegal-drug trade. Many drugs were coming into the United States from Panama. Manuel Noriega, the dictator of Panama, was involved in drug smuggling. On December 20, 1989, Bush sent U.S. troops to Panama, shown above, to arrest Noriega. He surrendered on January 3, 1990. Noriega was tried in a U.S. court and sent to prison.

1

The map on page 22 is of the country of Panama. The Caribbean Sea is to the north of Panama. The Pacific Ocean is to the south. Begin drawing your own map of Panama by making a rectangular guide.

2

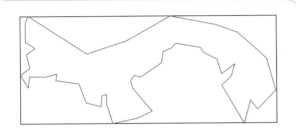

Look carefully at the drawing and use slanted lines to draw the guide for Panama.

3

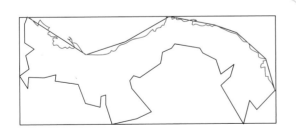

Use squiggly lines to fill in the northern coast of Panama. Look carefully at the drawing for help.

4

Look carefully at the drawing. Then use squiggly lines to finish drawing the shape of Panama.

5

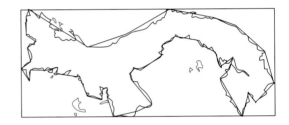

Draw nine islands off the coast of Panama. You can look at the drawing for help.

6

Erase all the guides from steps 1 and 2. Then shade in your map of Panama.

Operation Desert Storm

President George H. W. Bush faced another crisis on August 2, 1990, when Saddam Hussein, the 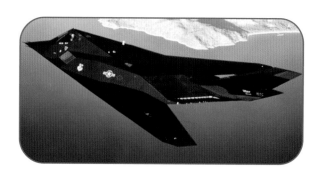 dictator of Iraq, sent his troops to take over the rich oil fields in Kuwait. Bush quickly formed an alliance of about 30 countries to stop Hussein. When Hussein refused to pull his troops out of Kuwait, the Persian Gulf War started on January 16, 1991. The war was also known as Operation Desert Storm. For almost six weeks, U.S. planes, such as the stealth bomber, shown here, pounded the Iraqi army with explosives. On February 24, 1991, U.S. soldiers entered Kuwait. The fighting lasted about 100 hours before the Iraqi army was driven out of Kuwait. On February 27, Bush announced that Kuwait was free.

After the success of Operation Desert Storm, President Bush's popularity increased. People welcomed the soldiers home with huge parades. However, within a few weeks, people began to fault Bush for not removing Hussein from power.

1

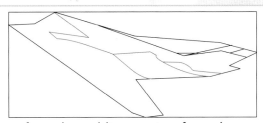

The picture of a stealth bomber on page 24 was taken in 1990, one year before the Persian Gulf War. Begin your drawing of the bomber with a rectangular guide.

2

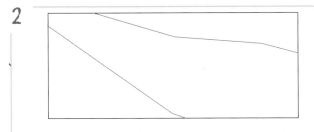

Draw five slanted lines as shown. The three top lines meet to form one long line. The other two slanted lines meet to form another long line.

3

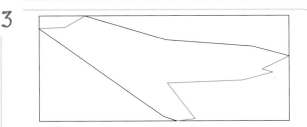

Draw two slanted lines in the left part of the box as shown. This is the front of the plane. Then add six more slanted lines to make the back of the plane as shown.

4

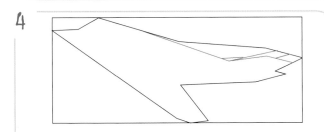

Add six slanted lines. Start with the longer lines and then add the shorter ones. You can look at the drawing for help.

5

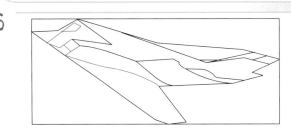

Draw four slanted lines going from the plane's front to its middle. Add a curved line connecting these lines to the plane's back. Add three slanted lines and two curved lines to the right as shown.

6

Add four slanted lines to make the window at the front of the plane. Add four more slanted lines to make the shape below the window. Draw a long curved line as shown.

7

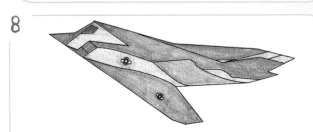

Erase the rectangular guide. Draw two small circles on the side of the plane. Add a star inside each circle. Look carefully at the drawing and add the shape around each circle.

8

Shade in your drawing of the stealth bomber. Remember to make the window dark and to leave the stars light.

National Problems

Despite President George H. W. Bush's success with foreign affairs, he was having problems closer to  home. When Bush had campaigned, he had promised not to raise taxes. However, the U.S. government needed more money. In 1990, Bush finally agreed to raise taxes. Many people were angry that he broke his campaign promise. Bush also vetoed, or stopped, a bill to raise the minimum wage because he felt it would hurt businesses.

Bush supported better protection for the environment. The importance of environmental protection was shown during the *Exxon Valdez* oil spill in Alaska on March 24, 1989. The oil ship crashed and about 11 million gallons (42 million l) of oil spilled, killing thousands of sea animals.

In 1992, President Bush ran for reelection. By this time his popularity was low because the U.S. economy was not doing well. Bush lost the election.

1

The big ship in the picture on page 26 is the *Exxon Valdez*. The tugboat is pulling it across Prince William Sound in Alaska in the spring of 1989. Begin your drawing of the boat with a rectangle.

2

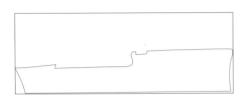

Draw a long slanted line at the bottom of the rectangle. Add curved lines to either end of the line. Look carefully at the drawing and add the curved and slanted lines above the long slanted line.

3

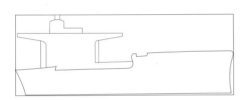

Draw a horizontal line in the left side of the rectangular guide. Add curved lines below it as shown. Add four vertical lines as shown. Draw the two shapes on top of the horizontal line. Add a slanted line to the right.

4

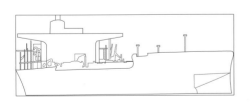

Add a curved line, a vertical line, and two slanted lines to the far right. Add the three tall T shapes on the right. Look carefully at the drawing and add the details around the shape you drew in step 3.

5

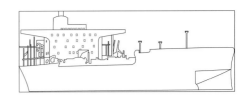

Add windows to the ship. Look carefully at the drawing for help. Notice that the windows are in five rows.

6

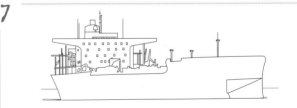

Draw the horizontal line across the top of the ship. Add the two small shapes above it. Draw six vertical lines on top of the ship. Add five small horizontal lines as shown.

7

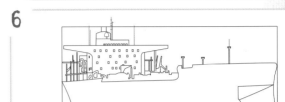

Erase the rectangular guide. Draw a horizontal line on each side of the ship for water. Add small wavy lines to the corners of the boat to show the water splashing against the boat.

8

Finish your picture of the *Exxon Valdez* with shading. The windows should all be dark.

The Retirement of the Forty-first President

George H. W. Bush was beaten by the Democrat Bill Clinton. When Clinton was sworn in on January 20, 1993, Bush and his wife returned to Houston, Texas. George H. W. Bush's son George W. Bush was elected president in 2000 and again in  2004. He is the second son of a president to become president himself.

As president Bush appointed many women to government positions. He also signed the Americans with Disabilities Act, which helped fight discrimination against people with disabilities. He signed bills to make the environment cleaner. He will best be remembered, though, as the president who fought against two dictators. He sent troops after Manuel Noriega to prevent more illegal drugs from entering the United States. He fought against Saddam Hussein to free the people of Kuwait.

1

The picture of George H. W. Bush on page 28 hangs in the National Portrait Gallery in Washington, D.C. Start your drawing of Bush by making a rectangular guide.

2

In the bottom right corner of the rectangular guide, draw a curved shape as shown. Add 11 slanted lines under the curving shape this line makes.

3

Draw an oval at the top of the rectangle as a guide for the president's head. Look carefully at the drawing and use slanted lines to draw the guide for his body.

4

Use wavy lines to draw his ears, his hair, his chin, and his neck as shown. Add three circles and a curved line as guides for his eyes, his nose, and his mouth.

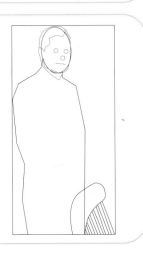

5

Use the guides to draw his eyes, his eyebrows, his nose, and his mouth as shown. Add wavy lines for the waves in his hair and the folds in his skin.

6

Draw the outline of Bush's body. Use wavy lines to draw both of his arms. Add the guides for his hands. Add curved lines for his tie, his collar, and the opening of his coat.

7

Draw his jacket collar and the bit of sleeve below his jacket. Draw his hands as shown. Add wavy lines to his jacket and the chair. Draw three ovals for buttons.

8

Erase all extra lines. You can now shade in your picture of President George H. W. Bush. His eyes, his hair, his tie, and the chair should all be dark.

Timeline

1924 George H. W. Bush is born in Milton, Massachusetts, on June 12.

1925 Bush's family moves to Greenwich, Connecticut.

1941 The United States enters World War II.

1942 Bush joins the U.S. Navy to fight in World War II.

1945 Bush and Barbara Pierce marry on January 6.

1948 Bush moves his family to Texas, where he works in the oil business.

1964 Bush loses the election for the U.S. Senate.

1966 Bush is elected to the U.S. House of Representatives.

1968 Bush is reelected to the House of Representatives.

1970 Bush loses the election for the U.S. Senate.

1971 President Nixon appoints Bush as U.S. ambassador to the United Nations.

1973 President Nixon appoints Bush as chairman of the Republican National Committee.

1974 President Ford appoints Bush as U.S. representative to China.

1976–1977 Bush serves as director of the Central Intelligence Agency.

1981–1989 Bush serves as vice president under President Ronald Reagan.

1988 Bush is elected as the forty-first president of the United States.

1989 Bush sends U.S. troops to Panama to arrest Manuel Noriega.

1990 Bush forms an alliance with more than 30 other nations to force Iraqi troops out of Kuwait.

1991 In the Persian Gulf War, U.S. soldiers beat Iraqi troops after four days of fighting.

1992 Bush loses the presidential election.

Glossary

alliance (uh-LY-unts) A group of countries working together toward a common goal.

ally (A-ly) A country that helps another country.

ambassador (am-BA-suh-der) An official who represents his or her country.

Central Intelligence Agency (SEN-trul in-TEH-lih-jints AY-jen-see) The U.S. government office that is in charge of spying on other countries.

committee (kuh-MIH-tee) A group of people directed to oversee or consider a matter.

Communist (KOM-yuh-nist) Belonging to a system in which all the land, houses, and factories belong to the government and are shared by everyone.

Democratic Party (deh-muh-KRA-tik PAR-tee) One of the two major political parties in the United States.

dictator (DIK-tay-ter) A person who takes power and has total control over others.

discrimination (dis-krih-muh-NAY-shun) Treating a person badly or unfairly just because he or she is different.

environment (en-VY-ern-ment) All the living things and conditions of a place.

foreign (FOR-in) Outside one's own country.

involved (in-VOLVD) Kept busy by something.

literacy (LIH-tuh-ruh-see) The ability to read and write.

minimum wage (MIH-nih-mum WAYJ) The lowest wage a worker can legally be paid.

pilot (PY-lut) A person who operates an aircraft, spacecraft, or large boat.

Republican Party (rih-PUH-blih-ken PAR-tee) One of the two major political parties in the United States.

resign (rih-ZYN) To step down from a position.

scandal (SKAN-dul) Conduct that people find shocking and bad.

senior (SEE-nyer) Having to do with the last year in high school or college.

smuggling (SMUH-gling) Sneaking something into or out of a place illegally.

stealth bomber (STELTH BAH-mer) An airplane that cannot be seen on radar.

symbol (SIM-bul) An object or a picture that stands for something else.

Index

Web Sites

Due to the changing nature of Internet links, PowerKids Press has developed an online list of Web sites related to the subject of this book. This site is updated regularly. Please use this link to access the list:
www.powerkidslinks.com/kgdpusa/ghwbush/